Each of Us
Will Never
Be the Same

Memories of
Charles Philip Price

Each of Us Will Never Be the Same

Memories of
Charles Philip Price

FORWARD MOVEMENT PUBLICATIONS
CINCINNATI, OHIO

Contents

Preface

I<small>T HAS BEEN SAID</small>, more than once, that no single individual had a greater influence on the Episcopal Church in the latter part of the twentieth century than Charles Philip Price.

Central architect of The Book of Common Prayer (1979) and The Hymnal (1982), Charlie's words, vigor, and theology have marked and changed the lives of countless numbers of the faithful.

It was of course his ability to change the lives of others by exposing them to his blinding passion for the life, death, and resurrection of Jesus Christ that makes Charles Philip Price so well remembered.

Remember was Charlie's favorite word. *Remember* in the sense not of a past event, long dead and forgotten, but *remember* as a powerful reality, so vibrant that it changed the world then and is more alive and active now than ever. Price traced the word in his doctoral dissertation, and it was the living essence of *remember* that marked Charles Price's teaching and his life.

The very few, eloquent memories that are in this small book are gathered from what could have been literally hundreds of testimonials of how one Christian life impacted others. As but one of those lives, I need say again that *"Each of us will never be the same."*

Charles Philip Price changed lives. He changed hundreds of them, and the power and presence of the man we now *remember* changes lives today. He does so through all that he has said and done for us in the name of Jesus Christ. It is all summed up, made clear, in Charlie's powerful words, *A General Thanksgiving*, that appears on page 836 of The Book of Common Prayer.

Accept, O Lord, our thanks and praise for all that you have done for us. We thank you for the splendor of the whole creation, for the beauty of this world, for the wonder of life, and for the mystery of love.

We thank you for the blessing of family and friends, and for the loving care which surrounds us on every side.

We thank you for setting us at tasks which demand our best efforts, and for leading us to accomplishments which satisfy and delight us.

We thank you also for those disappointments and failures that lead us to acknowledge our dependence on you alone.

Above all, we thank you for your Son Jesus Christ; for the truth of his Word and the example of his life; for his steadfast obedience, by which he overcame temptation; for his dying, through which he overcame death; and for his rising to life again, in which we are raised to the life of your kingdom.

Grant us the gift of your Spirit, that we may know Christ and make him known; and through him, at all times and in all places, may give thanks to you in all things. Amen.

A Minister Remembered:
Charles Philip Price, '41: The Harvard Years

WHEN GEORGE ARTHUR BUTTRICK retired in 1960 as the sixth Plummer Professor of Christian Morals and Preacher to the University, President Nathan Marsh Pusey set about the daunting task of seeking his successor. In a three-year interim period the daily affairs of The Memorial Church were placed in the hands of an acting minister who reported directly to Pusey and the Board of Preachers, while, as he had in so many of the appointments which, since 1953, had virtually recreated the Divinity faculty, the president served as his own search committee, seeking wide counsel but reserving the appointment to himself.

His choice was The Reverend Charles Philip Price, a graduate of Harvard College in the Class of 1941, an Episcopal priest, and a teacher of systematic theology in the Virginia Theological Seminary. At forty-three, Price was one of the youngest men ever to serve in the preachership: in college he had been in the Eliot House, and had graduated summa cum laude with a concentration in mathematics. He had served in the navy in World War II, been ordained a priest in 1949 after study at Virginia Seminary, and in 1962, had received his Th.D. from Union Theological Seminary.

Nathan Pusey was one of the nation's most conspicuous Episcopal laymen, and while his appointment of co-religionist Price was without controversy, both men were sensitive to the charge that Harvard's chapel, long

nourished in the Unitarian and Congrega-
tional traditions, could seem now to be in alien
hands. Price asked the president what would
be appropriate dress for the conduct of the
Sunday services, aware that the traditional
Anglican garb of cassock, surplice, and scarf
might put people off. As he told the story,
Charlie had consulted Mr. Pusey, who sent
him to Bishop Anson Phelps Stokes. The
Bishop, demurring, sent him to Ted Ferris,
who "knew everything." Ferris gave Price a
splendid lunch in one of his Boston clubs, and
said, "The Prayer Book is silent on vesture.
Wear what you please." Charlie did, and was
always seen in his black Union doctoral gown
and clerical collar.

Price had hardly settled into his first term,
in the fall of 1963, when he was confronted
with the greatest domestic crisis since the
war, the assassination of President Kennedy
on November 22, 1963. Anyone alive then
remembers the national trauma of those days,
and Harvard felt the loss more accurately than
most. It fell to the new preacher to orches-
trate the University's public grief, and he did
so in an austere memorial service in The

Memorial Church on November 23rd, with twelve hundred squeezed into the pews, more than three hundred standing, and eight hundred more outside in silence. "Once he was here, walking the same streets which you and I walk, sitting in the same classrooms, perhaps reading the same books in Widener," Price said in his eulogy; "Now he had died for his country, and we died a little when he died." He widened the circle of grief when, in consideration of the sniper who had cut down the sixth son of Harvard to become president of the United States, he asked, "Can we find room for pity?"

Thus, early on and at a visible and tragic moment, Price established his reputation as a candid, compassionate and prophetic voice unafraid to preach across the bow of conventional wisdom. He felt that his ancient title of "Preacher to the University" not only permitted him to do so but compelled him; and his address was widely reprinted in the national press.

As Preacher to the University, Price inherited a wide range of duties, including administrative charge of the church, and service as chairman of the Board of Preachers and of the Faculty Committee on Phillips Brooks House, which had a long and close relationship with the College chapel. He shared in the counsels of the Faculty of Divinity and of Arts and Sciences, where he also taught; and he took a role of advocacy in the United Ministry to students. Widely sought as counselor to both students and faculty, he maintained a full schedule of weddings, baptisms, funerals, and memorial services.

Along with all of this, Charlie served as a member of the liturgical commission of the Episcopal Church, where his informed scholarship eventuated in The Book of Common Prayer 1979, which succeeded that of 1928. He also served on the committee to revise the 1940 Episcopal hymnal.

While eager to preserve the best influences of The Memorial Church in a time of change and conflict, Dr. Price was equally committed to making the church responsive to the pressing issues of the day, and one of the ways he achieved this was by broadening the franchise of its pulpit. Keenly interested in the ecumenical movement and its relationship to change in the Roman Catholic Church as a consequence of Vatican II, Dr. Price invited, as the first Noble Lecturer in his tenure, Dr. Willem Adolph Visser't Hoofe, Secretary of the World Council of Churches. Early in the following year he organized Harvard's first observance of the Week of Prayer for Christian Unity in cooperation with the United Ministry, the Divinity faculty and the bishop of the Greek Orthodox Church. In 1964 he secured Cardinal Cushing's permission for Roman Catholics at Harvard to participate as speakers in the services of Daily Prayers in Appleton Chapel and Roman Catholic weddings to take place in The Memorial Church, permission for which had hitherto been denied by the archdiocese. In 1966 he invited the first Roman Catholic priest to preach at a Sunday morning service, The Reverend John Courtney Murray, S.J., of Woodstock College in Maryland. In 1971 Price broke the gender barrier with his invitation to Professor Mary Daly of Boston College to preach, on which occasion she delivered her memorable address "Beyond God the Father," and led the walk-out which became one of the defining moments of the feminists movement.

Dr. Price extended the hospitality of The Memorial Church for the celebration of the Jewish Holy Days in September 1966, starting a Harvard tradition which extends to this day. Rabbis were invited to participate in the annual ecumenical thanksgiving services, and they routinely accepted Price's invitations to speak at Daily Prayers.

Also in 1966, at the height of the anti-war movement and in a period of great difficulty for Price, for whom patriotism and conscience were not mutually exclusive, he invited Senator Eugene McCarthy to preach on a Sunday, and to deliver the Noble Lectures on three successive evenings. McCarthy took as his topic "Religion and Politics," and Price moderated the discussions in a church filled to capacity. In May 1967 he devoted a Sunday sermon to the war, in which he both opposed the war and affirmed the responsibility to serve in it if called. "I have a lot of sympathy with men whose consciences will not allow them to go," he said, "but to be quite honest, I can't raise my conscience to that pitch of sensitivity. I believe that the state has a right to ask military service of its citizens." Unlike many preachers of the day, Price recognized the ambiguity of his own position: his notion was that the preacher's obligation is not to find easy or even agreeable solutions but, in a mixed and fallen world, to struggle to make as much sense as possible out of an inevitable moral ambiguity.

In January 1965, Charles Price invited Martin Luther King, Jr., to preach in The Memorial Church. Every seat was filled an hour before the service, the sermon was broadcast into Sanders Theatre, and that evening Price sponsored a public lecture by Dr. King at Rindge Technical High School. Price was one of King's earliest and most visible supporters in the Boston area, and very much involved in matters of racial reconciliation: in April 1968 he conducted a memorial service for King.

At the time of the University's own internal crisis of April 1969, when students seized University Hall, evicted the deans and were themselves later rousted by the police, Price opened the doors of the church to accommodate the traumatized student groups, thereby becoming one of the few establishment figures to whom people of conflicting opinions would listen.

In 1964 he presided over the creation of a hymn book, the first new Harvard University Hymn Book since 1927; and in 1967 Charles Price presided over the installation of a remarkable new organ, at the time the largest American-built tracker action instrument. His own keen interest and competence in music made him a natural ally of musicians, and his enthusiastic hymn singing on Sunday mornings was legendary. Charlie wrote or adapted many new hymns now included in the Episcopal Hymnal 1982.

In 1972, after nine years service, the last five as Plummer Professor of Christian Morals, Charlie gave his resignation to then President Derek Bok in order to return to Virginia Seminary, which for two years had been holding a chair for him in theology. In an open letter to the congregation he wrote, "I've come to the conclusion that my interests and abilities do...lie in teaching, training men for the ministry and throwing in my lot with denominational theological education at a time of considerable crisis." In modest self-evaluation of his time in The Memorial Church, he said, "I would like to think that I have been able to bring some balance, openness, and compassion to bear on our life here during the past nine years." He had inherited a complex job as preacher, teacher, and administrator, and he acknowledged that the Church had not been immune to the general decline in college religious life which was then epidemic across America. If one were to try to fight that trend, he thought, such a job description should be revised to permit more attention to the institutional life of the Church, which would of necessity compromise the teaching aspect; and such a prospect would not be agreeable to him. Dr. Price left for Virginia with the deep appreciation and affection of a host of admirers among students, faculty, alumni, and friends of the University.

Charles Price had a life before he came to Harvard in 1963, and he returned to it with great vigor after his resignation. His second career at Virginia Seminary, from 1972 to 1997, as systematic theologian, scholar of liturgies and pastoral theology, poet, and musician, found him at the center of the work of his church, and there, by precept and example, he shaped an entire generation's priesthood. Nathan Pusey, in a recent memoir, described Charles Price as, "The most

Memories of Charles P. Price

intellectual member of the Episcopal Church in the last twenty-five years." He continued, "He's the kind of minister I like…The years he was at Harvard, you could just feel him grow. He learned to adapt the Christian mission to that intense intellectual community which is Harvard. We're filled with every kind of doubter and skeptic you can get. He found a way to talk constructively. He was a brilliant guy."

Charles Philip Price died in October 1999 in the eightieth year of his age. He is buried at Virginia Seminary. Those of us who knew and loved Charlie will ever remember his infectious laugh, his robust singing, his vigorous preaching, his loyalty to the church and his passion for honesty and truth.

— *Peter J. Gomes*

When the News
Came . . . I Cried

Wʜᴇɴ ᴛʜᴇ ɴᴇᴡs ᴄᴀᴍᴇ that Charles Price had died, I cried. Since September 1960, when I entered the Virginia Seminary, Charles had been a very important figure in my life. He was my advisor while at VTS and he provided the premarital counseling for my wife Sarah and me. He presided at our wedding service, preached the homily and celebrated the Eucharist for us, in the Seminary Chapel.

Growing up in a small farming town in southern New Jersey, being the only one in my family to attend college, was to leave me unprepared for the likes of the teachers I encountered at VTS. To have Mollegan, Stanley, Booty, Newman, and Price nearly constantly for three years took a lot of getting used to. The notion of "keeping up" with these folks was breathtaking and I am not sure that I ever managed to do so.

I suppose that three words, for me, most adequately frame the influence of Charles Price. Intensity is the first: no one, in my experience, brought such intensity to his teaching. My one clear recollection after class with him, be it Systematics or Liturgics or Forsythe, was a great tiredness. How could anyone have that much energy for that topic, that subject, and sustain that level of energy? And he managed, most of the time, to make that topic, that subject, interesting and important. That trait, making it interesting, was a fundamental part of his power as a teacher. Somehow it seemed that if Charles Price was interested, then it was likely to be interesting. Certainly his interest in liturgics and his teaching of liturgics has been an enduring influence in my life as a priest. It made it possible to endure all the fuss when the BCP of 1979 appeared. He encouraged me, by his example, to always be focused, to be centered in the teaching moment.

The second word has to do with preparation. If Charles was ever unprepared, I never knew it. No matter the day, the circumstances, the events in the larger world around us, he seemed prepared. And by that example, encouraged me to imitate him. Have I done it? Likely not on an everyday basis, but I have always known what I could and should have done. He became a kind of canon, a measuring stick. I have come out of the pulpit on more than one occasion and said to myself, "That was not a good piece of work. Dr. Price would send you back to do that one over! You did not do nor finish the prep work." And I would later take the time to rework the piece. As the sign in the print shop said: "There's never time to do it right, but there's always time to do it over."

And the third way in which he has deeply influenced me is that he was nearly always lucid. I think one of the most startling things he said in Liturgics was, "For the first five years in the parish ministry, do not break any of the rubrics. Then, when you break one, be sure you know why!" So always, to the degree possible, be clear! Be clear with yourself and with others. Always be ready to explain. And he strove for clarity in his teaching, in his homiletical work, and in his social interactions. Most certainly, Charles stood ready to explain himself to anyone who asked.

A most enduring image, for me, is the photo of Charles in the Holy Land. In a procession, ready to go forward or already in motion, his head up and his mouth seemingly filled with the words of the hymn that was to be sung. If it was Easter, I hope that the hymn was Brian Wren's, "Christ is alive!" (1982, #182). For no particularly clear reason, this Easter hymn catches much that I have come to treasure because of the influence of Charles P. Price in my life. He was a teacher, Rabbinic of the first class. Higher praise I cannot express. May he go from strength to strength in the realms of Light and Glory.

— *Richard H. Lewis*

Life is the Greatest
of All Experiences

My FIRST ENCOUNTER with Charlie Price was in October 1946 on the second floor of Aspinwall Hall at Virginia Seminary. We had been assigned as roommates along with Henry Seaman and would share a bedroom and a study for our first two years of seminary. Henry and I had just met and were standing speculating on this Charles Price assigned as our third roommate when suddenly through the door strode Charlie. There was not a doubt in my mind at this first meeting with Charlie that this fellow was a man of enormous energy, openness, and interesting possibilities. The years that followed bore out the truth of that in spades. Charlie never did anything except with passion and excellence, be it sailing, driving, playing the piano, studying, preaching, teaching, walking, and discussing theology, politics, or human affairs.

His deeply grounded faith in his Lord was transparent in everything he was and anything he did. He was faithful to a fault in his daily times of prayer and meditation as well as his participation in the life and activity of whatever parish's life he shared. His presentation of the gospel in preaching and teaching came out of his passionate engagement of spirit and mind with the Holy Scriptures and the wisdom of the great theological figures from all of Christian history—as well as with that gospels' relevance to present, personal human affairs. This deeply endeared him with all whom he both challenged and enlightened in university, seminary, parish, or wherever. His passion lit fires in the minds and hearts of his hearers which emerged in them in their own witnessing and living out of the faith. What a model of Christian living he was! "He was the fairest of men, grace flowed from his lips for God has blessed him forever" (Ps 45:2). That verse from the psalms captured some of the wonder of Charlie.

The courage of this man in facing the great hurts and sorrows of his life was awesome to behold. When Betty and he lost their daughter Emily at age 6, who but Charlie conducted the Burial Office? (At the conclusion of which he recited the childhood prayer he used nightly over the years with her and her sister.) Then, in his latter years when he was fighting cancer, some of us recall personally how, while wearing an onerous medical appliance, he led as chaplain the meditations of our diocesan council. Many or most of the folks present on that occasion never realized under what a burden he offered his evocative thoughts. Later, within weeks of his death, I watched him stand up to deliver a Lenten presentation in his parish on the doctrine of the Trinity. I marveled that he could speak over his great discomfort and disability in a way that riveted the attention of his listeners. His obvious faith and intense passion won the day.

As one prep school student once wrote in an English essay, "Life is the greatest of all experiences." Charlie was a lover of life and everything in it. Charlie loved the church of his Lord but never uncritically. He wanted it to be the best possible agent both in its worship and in its service to the world. He always put his actions where his traveling was, his money where his mouth was. He cherished the wonders and beauty of all creation and, in his later years, environmental concerns received his whole-hearted attention. In his own version of a General Thanksgiving he wrote: "We thank you for the splendor of the whole creation, for the beauty of this world, for the wonder of life, and for the mystery of love." He and Betty lived out their concern for creation with their thoughtful management of their property on the northern neck of Virginia by buying up small patches of wetland which they feared might be taken over for development.

Music was a deeply cherished part of his life, from his early years in a parish's boy choir right up to his end in this life. He had a good voice as an adult, well-exhibited in the seminary choir and the seminary's student production of Gilbert and Sullivan operettas. He was an accomplished pianist and at a time entertained the possibility of that as a career. The Prices, wherever they were, were supporters of the community's musical organizations; in Washington of its opera and the National Cathedral's musical programs. It was the same in the world of art. Their home had significant paintings and *objects d'art* from a wide variety of periods, some of museum quality. Charlie's love of the arts was strong, varied and discriminating.

There was hardly anything in life to which Charlie did not give himself with that intensity and passion that so marked his personality and endeared him to all whose lives crossed his path. When Charlie was around, life was always exciting no matter the occasion. I myself was greatly blessed that I enjoyed his friendship from that first meeting at Virginia Seminary in 1946 right up to the day he died in 1999. The way he lived out his life of faith enkindled in me a desire for me to be as much myself by God's grace as he was himself.

"Grant us the gift of your Spirit, that we may know Christ and make him known; and through him, at all times and in all places, may give thanks to you in all things. *Amen*."

— *Philip A. Smith*

The Teacher of
a Lifetime

Charles Philip Price is my most important teacher. He influenced what I learned,
why I learned, and increased my desire to learn.
I took every course he offered during my years
at Virginia Seminary—eight of them. No one
is perfect, but Charles Price embodied the
height and depth and beauty, the joy and the
pain of the Christian faith. A teacher of pro-
found ability, he modeled what he proclaimed.

Charlie's doctoral degree was in Old
Testament. His faculty appointment was

Systematic Theology, and he also taught Christian Thought, Homiletics, Speech, and Music. He lectured with vigor and compassion, often embodying the person of whom he spoke, until he broke from the role, walked down from the podium to stand in front of the class and speak as Charles Price.

Tertullian was his topic the first time I remember that Charlie did this. Standing directly in front of us, looking deadly serious, he shook a commendatory finger and said, "Remember Tertullian. Remember Tertullian. He had a bright idea. It's called the Trinity. Someday you may have a bright idea."

Lecturing on the Psalms, he came to Psalm 103. "As for mortals, their days are like grass; they flourish like a flower of the field; for the wind passes over it, and it is gone, and its place knows it no more."

Down from the podium, finger aloft, moving rapidly, "You remember that," he said. "Remember that. And if you ever doubt it, you come back here, come back in five years, just five years, and see if anyone remembers your name."

Of course, when we did return in five years, or whenever, one person remembered our names and everything else about us— Charlie Price.

Charlie's greatest impact as a teacher for me was in his course on Liturgics. There is little doubt that over a period of twenty-five years Price's contributions to The Book of Common Prayer (1979) and The Hymnal (1982) left the greatest mark on the life of the Episcopal Church made by any single individual during that important and significant period of change and new life. What Charlie taught me in his course, Liturgics, was appreciation and understanding of the height and depth of Christian worship, as it has been shaped in the Anglican communion.

Liturgics led on in the next semester to an elective course in the Theology of the Sacraments. Early in this semester, Charlie's younger daughter died tragically. The Senior Class gathered in the choir of the Seminary Chapel, not knowing who would conduct the service, until Charlie started down the aisle with the small white casket, "I am the resurrection and the life." He read the full text of

First Corinthians, chapter fifteen, and concluded with the prayer, now a part of the liturgy, "A sheep of thine own fold, a lamb of thine own redeeming."

The next morning a small group of us gathered for his course in the sacraments, uncertain if he would appear. When he did, he said: "Thank you for your prayers and your presence yesterday in Chapel. If any of you would like to talk with me about what happened, I shall try to respond. Meanwhile, it is important that I teach. I am first of all a teacher. If my work becomes more difficult than I can bear, I shall be the first to let you know. Now, let us turn to the material of the day."

Three years after graduation, I was in the Seminary Refectory for lunch one spring day, when I saw a familiar face, Nathan Pusey, President of Harvard, who had traveled to Alexandria to ask Charlie to serve as Preacher to the University. Charlie accepted the offer and became a great friend of President Pusey; however, Charlie often said he never would have done it had not Pusey come to see him in person.

When Charles Price returned to the Seminary in 1972, *The Boston Globe* published a long article describing his Harvard tenure. Charlie was typically self-effacing in the interview, speaking of what he might have done better. I sat down and wrote him a letter saying that no one could have done it better, and I knew whereof I wrote. "You changed my life." Price replied in a hand-written note, "I have always maintained that I deal not in quantity but quality. You merely prove my point."

In 1987, when I was asked to join the Seminary faculty as Director of Development, I consulted Charlie before making my decision. He wrote, remembering what Angus Dun had said to him when he was considering Pusey's offer to go to Harvard. "No one can tell another what to do," Dun, who knew both Harvard and the Seminary, had said to Price, "But I think you ought to do it." Then said Price to Gleason, "I think you ought to do it."

The last time I heard Charlie preach was at Cliff Stanley's Burial. Cliff had been Charlie's teacher, model, mentor. The text

Charlie chose was Genesis 6:4. "It was a time when giants walked the earth." Without a doubt, the words fitted Cliff. So too, they described the preacher.

There was no way, none, that Charles Price was not a giant: teacher, preacher, pastor, priest, friend, mentor, model, thoroughly married and deeply loyal to those matters and meanings central to his life that were many. He was consistent and natural, skilled with words and music, the language of science and the soul. In my life experience I have known no one who is his equal.

Charlie was fond of speaking of "The Price Comma," an important emendation in the Nicene Creed of the 1979 Book of Common Prayer. The Price Comma, however, is not nearly as important as the Price Rubric, the Easter Rubric that Charlie wrote and appended to the Burial of the Dead. These are the words that sum up the life of Charles Philip Price. May they be true for each of us.

— *Edward S. Gleason*

NOTE:

The liturgy for the dead is an Easter liturgy. It finds all its meaning in the resurrection. Because Jesus was raised from the dead, we too shall be raised.

The liturgy, therefore, is characterized by joy, in the certainty that "neither death, nor life, nor angels, nor principalities, nor things present, nor things to come, nor powers, nor height, nor depth, nor anything else in all creation, will be able to separate us from the love of God in Christ Jesus our Lord."

This joy, however, does not make human grief unChristian. The very love we have for each other in Christ brings deep sorrow when we are parted by death. Jesus himself wept at the grave of his friend. So, while we rejoice that one we love has entered the nearer presence of our Lord, we sorrow in sympathy with those who mourn.

—The Book of Common Prayer
Page 507

John the Baptist

W HAT I MOST ADMIRED about Charlie was his determination to commit himself to all avenues of ministry to which he was called. Yes, he was a teacher, scholar, musician, poet, preacher, counselor, and mentor, but also much more. Thus, we sometimes forget about his service to the Church—in his parish, on committees of his diocese, as long-time Deputy to General Convention, in which he was Chaplain to the House of Deputies, and as chair or member of numerous commissions and task forces appointed by the Presiding Bishop or the General Convention. In all, he was, as I say, committed. To borrow a familiar phrase from the sports world, Charlie "always came to play."

I sometimes am asked to present the canons of the Church to a newly-installed member of the clergy (or laity) as part of a service in Celebration of New Ministry (BCP, p. 559). I get up and say, "*N.N.,* obey these Canons," and there is a good-natured titter in the congregation, which would be fine if it didn't drown out the rest—and most important part—of the Prayer Book's intended admonition—"and be among us to share in the counsels of this diocese." Charlie understood that admonition—as he did so much of the Prayer Book—and accepted the call in ways that few of us do, both within the academic community and without. In my view, it was Charlie at his best. He brought all his intellect, scholarship and decency to the table and shared them.

Charlie at his most fun, of course, was the man of wit and mirth—usually accompanied by his huge, enveloping, laugh. But he wasn't always like that. Once upon a time, I learned that Charlie and Phil Smith (former Bishop of New Hampshire and Suffragan of Virginia) had roomed together at Virginia Seminary. I was eager to find out what that collegial experience was like and especially whether it was fun. And so, I asked Phil one evening at a reception at the Seminary what it was like to room with Charlie, and he bellowed in response, "O God, it was awful—it was like living with John the Baptist!"

I wonder how many of us envy Phil!

— David Booth Beers

Grasped by God

By the time I arrived at Virginia Seminary in 1978, Charlie Price was already a legend. In a time of many remarkable teachers, Charlie was that and more. Students referred to his classes with something like awe. I had heard of an earlier era at the Seminary when giants still bestrode the earth bearing names such as Molly and Cliff. Charlie seemed to be a hold-over from those days of glory—a giant still among us.

Charlie was oblivious to the admiration. I remember in talks with classmates marveling at his passion and intellectual rigor coupled with his extraordinary humility. Having come to seminary from several years as a graduate student, I knew how rare such a combination of gifts is.

He was an unforgettable teacher. Given the luck of the draw, my class did not have him for his signature course—his two semester systematic theology survey. I had heard repeatedly that this was the most lucid and moving presentation of the Christian faith anyone had ever heard. Somehow, in most ways lost to me now, I was able to borrow a set of tapes of Charlie's lectures for the course from a student in the class ahead. And I still remember driving for hours back from Mississippi listening to his lucid, impassioned presentation on ultimate concern, being, the Jesus of history and the Christ of faith, human spirit and Holy Spirit.

Every lecture began with an outline on the blackboard. Charlie's mathematical mind had everything rigorously organized. He would begin with careful exposition and then, more often than not, at some point his presentation would take off in an explosion of insight. Charlie loved Paul Tillich's (his mentor) metaphor of being "grasped" by God's

Spirit. I was "grasped" more times than I can count as I sat in many classes at the Seminary, but with Charlie it was a nearly daily occurrence.

Twice I took reading courses with Charlie, on Tillich's *Systematic Theology* and, later on Karl Rahner's *Foundations of Christian Faith*. In both I was able to witness Charlie's mind probing, wondering, challenging. He had never read Rahner before, so a fellow student, Ellen Alston, and I took the plunge with him. Ellen and I liked Rahner more than he did, as I recall. Charlie's Protestant instincts resisted the Roman Catholic theologian's approach. "God is first of all for me a *power* word," Charlie said, less at home with Rahner's emphasis on knowledge and mystery. In those lively afternoon sessions in the study at his home it was those conversations with a first-rate theological mind and a generous, searching spirit that took me to new places.

Charlie showed me what great preaching could be. He focused his fiery mind on the text, took it with absolute seriousness, and then preached lucidly and passionately. He never kept files of sermon illustrations, he told me, and he didn't use a wealth of anecdote and story. But you had a sense in hearing him that someone was speaking out of the depths directly to your own depths. He had been grasped by God, and as you listened it was quite likely that you would be, too. It could shake your foundations.

Few of us will ever forget his sermon for Wednesday in Holy Week on Judas and the mystery of iniquity. And the best articulation I have ever heard of the meaning of the cross came from three sermons Charlie preached on Good Friday at the National Cathedral. Charlie was always generous in giving copies of his sermons, most of them still in hand-written form. I go back to them often.

For all his intensity, one of Charlie's trade-marks was his laughter. He loved to tell funny stories, and when he did he always laughed louder and longer than anyone else. Those of us who were around him heard the best stories more than once. One of the last of his lectures I read was on Sydney Smith, the eighteenth century Anglican priest and humorist. Charlie loved his wit and his delight in mocking the foibles of the world around him. For him, deep faith and an enthusiastic sense of humor belonged together.

In our senior year Charlie taught our class Liturgics, which, given his low church predilections, was really a course on the history of the Prayer Book. I remember two things from those lectures in Sparrow Hall to a group of increasingly restless seniors ready to take on the church. One was his cherished themes— his love of the Anglican spirit of compromise, of our balanced heritage both Catholic and Protestant (though we knew where his heart was), and of the vast resource of communal and personal devotion encapsulated in our Book of Common Prayer through all its revisions.

The other was an electric moment that continues to influence my ministry. Charlie was making a point I've now forgotten related to some of the new 1979 Prayer Book practices. Having finished his point as he paced briskly around the platform in the front of Sparrow Hall, he all of a sudden seemed to take flight. He jumped up in the air, both feet for a moment tucked beneath him, and then his feet came crashing down on the hard wooden platform. "Now listen to me," he demanded. "All these new things our worship is reclaiming are important. But don't you forget to love those people you serve! Don't be harsh with them. Lead them carefully. Help them to understand."

I have never forgotten that. In it is Charlie's commitment to the church's faithful witness, but also his care for the individual parishioners who make up our parish communities.

It is hard to believe he is gone. His presence at the Seminary was vital and intense for so long. I miss his passion for Christ, for handing on the faith to his students, for teaching us the discipline of loving God with all our heart and mind. Charlie had them both— heart and mind. And his grandeur of mind and spirit continues to inspire those of us who were given the gift of knowing him.

— *Samuel T. Lloyd*

The Faith Upon
Which I Have
Built My Life

THIS IS A LETTER to Charles P. Price from a person who considers himself blessed to have known Charlie for almost thirty years as teacher, mentor, and friend.

Dear Charlie,

You had just returned to Virginia Seminary the year before we of the class of 1977 arrived, and so we were the first class to have you for three whole years in your second tour of duty on the "holy hill." I remember very well the fall retreat that first year, when our class asked you to be our "faculty advisor." At some point in the weekend you and I took a long walk in the woods, enjoying the turning of the leaves and beginning a conversation that would continue, on and off, until your death. Like so many others, I am deeply grateful for everything you gave me through the years, and I want to say something about each of the roles you played in my life—teacher, mentor, and friend.

Your reputation as a teacher proceeded you, and we wondered if it could possibly be true, that you were *that* good. The reports were accurate. There were many days when it was hard to tell whether we had heard a lecture or an extended homily. There were times when the entire class spontaneously burst into applause at the end of the hour. However, it was not the presentation that has stayed with me all these years, but the substance of what you taught us. I doubt that a week goes by even now that I do not quote you. My Bible study class is probably weary of hearing the words, "As my friend and mentor Charlie Price used to say…." Not long ago my clergy staff and I were having a theological discussion about the parish's policies on Baptism and reception of the Eucharist. I told them that you had taught us that "God is not bound by the sacraments, but we are." It turned the conversation on its ear and helped us reach the consensus we needed. I know there are ministers, lay and ordained, in congregations across the country (and around the world) who can tell similar stories about how your teaching has formed their teaching and theology.

A great deal of what I learned from you, and what has become the foundation of my priestly ministry, was not communicated in the classroom, and that is why I also call you my mentor. We sat next to each other in chapel almost every morning for three years. I would get there early because I had been out walking and saying my prayers in the woods. In my mind's eye I can hear the back door of the chapel open and your distinctive footsteps come up the side aisle, and you would slip into "our" pew. I would glance over, catch your eye, and you would nod ever so slightly. I did not learn much about liturgical ceremonial at VTS; but, sitting next to you in chapel all those days, I learned to love the liturgy, and I learned to pray it rather than just read it. In that sense, you continue to sit next to me every Sunday morning. Your spiritual counsel has been a part of my pastoral ministry in ways I can hardly begin to describe. I remember the day we were having lunch in the refectory and were "abstractly" discussing life in the Kingdom, most specifically whether or not only human beings were going to participate. All of a sudden it got personal. I told you about Curly, my family's dog, who during many years of my adolescence was literally the only friend I thought I had. One day, when he was dying, he tried to crawl up into my lap. I had on a pair of new pants and did not want his hair all over them, so I turned him away. The next day he died when I was at school. I told you that my rejection of him had haunted me for years, and I asked you if the Kingdom had anything to do with that kind of loss. You told me that the Kingdom would not be the consummation of all things for me if it did not include Curly bounding over a hill and into my arms, with all forgiven. You said you did not know exactly how it was going to work, but somehow it was what was meant by God bringing about a new heaven *and* a new earth. You taught so many of us how to keep our eyes open wider than we thought we could to the possibilities of God's grace and mercy.

I hope I am not being presumptuous in also calling you my friend. I didn't know what you would say when I first asked you to join me for tea in my room in St. George's Hall. You came that day, much to the surprise of my floor mates, and over the next three years we shared many an hour of theological conversation that covered novels and movies and the history of our families. When I was getting ready to return to California for ordination and the beginning of a new ministry at Grace Cathedral in San Francisco, I told you that I was concerned about what the distance would do to our friendship. You told me that "the ground between us will be holy ground," and that God would work out the rest. As it turned out, the time between us was holy time. We would see each other every few years when I came to VTS for the Fall Convocation. We would sit next to each other in chapel and it was as if no time had passed at all. We would share a meal and a bottle of wine, and it was as if the conversation had never been interrupted. Among so many other things, you taught me that friendship in Christ is built upon a foundation that neither time nor distance can destroy.

Charlie, all the great mentors in my life are dead now. John deBoer Cummings, my childhood priest, Stanley Forrest Rodgers, the Dean of Grace Cathedral, my parents, and you. If you had not taught me as you did, if you had not shared your life and yourself with me as you did, I could feel bereft and alone, in the deepest spiritual sense. But the grace of the faith upon which I have built my life, and the hope in the resurrection that I cling to like a lifeboat, are due in great part to my knowing you and sitting at your feet. I long for the day when I will gaze upon your face once again. I praise God for all you were to us, and give thanks that God chose to create such a teacher, mentor, and friend as you.

Faithfully yours,
— David Walton Miller

Jesus Tender
Shepherd Hear Me

WHEN TED GLEASON WROTE to me asking that I contribute to a Forward Movement remembrance of Charlie Price my initial thought was, "What might I add that has not already been expressed by so many about this remarkable individual?" Charlie's place in the history of the church in general and the Episcopal Church in particular was more than adequately summed up by The Very Rev. Richard Reid at Charlie's funeral on October 18, 1999 when he proclaimed: "Today we must add Charlie Price's name to the list of giants, the giants of intellect, courage, faithfulness, skill in teaching and preaching, and care and concern for all God's people…."

Here are several reflections about this giant that I am pleased to offer.

The copious notes that I took during the classes I was privileged to have under his tutelage are no longer in my files after these forty plus years since seminary. But I do remember some practical advice he shared during a liturgics class. Charlie opined that when going to a new parish always respect their tradition. After all, the people in the pews have been there a lot longer than you. In the recent era of great change in liturgical practices this was not always easy to do, but necessary to keep in mind as one worked through the "new" Prayer Book, that he was so instrumental in helping to compile. And an additional word from Charlie, at the same time, was always treat the altar with care, be definite in your actions. His words about this were something like "don't be sloppy"—not terribly theological but certainly practical.

In my files I did find a sermon Charlie preached on the Tuesday before Advent

(November 26, 1957). This was during the first semester of my first year at Virginia Seminary. His opening words were, "This sermon has for its text the entire book of Joel." Charlie picked up on the thought that the entire book is a liturgy for Judgment Day, and he posed the question, "Is not a liturgy for Judgment Day particularly appropriate for our day?" In once again rereading his words, I have to offer a resounding "Yes"—not only for the fall of 1957, but for the present as well. For Joel, the present event that inspired this liturgy was a plague of locusts. Charlie pointed to "two locust plagues which trouble us: one is the internal struggle for civil rights...the other...the drawing apart of the nations into two hostile camps (the Non-Communist and Communist political arenas)." Substitute the internal struggles for integrity in business practices and the continuing concerns for the homeless and other human needs in the present day United States, and the external threat of terrorist activity and the possible assault of weapons of mass destruction, and the sermon is preachable today. Charlie not only pointed to the issues for Judgment Day, but also clearly expressed the hope with which

Christians are endowed, and he raised the question: Can the Church summon the Nation to repentance? "I do not know," is his honest homiletic response. "Your ministries and mind will provide part of the answer. I do know this. We should learn to do so, if we want to be true to the Biblical understanding of our calling." In the grand scheme of things one person's ministry often does not reach very far; but I kept that sermon for a reason. One has to have a vision, and his words were one important ingredient that I have tried to incorporate in my vision of ministry.

A final word. In his funeral sermon for Charlie, Reid added a very important point in his litany reflecting Charlie's gifts of character, and that was his care and concern for others. Charlie and Betty knew deep personal tragedy when their daughter Emily died. During her funeral, at which he officiated, he prayed the hymn, "Jesus tender Shepherd hear me, Bless the little lambs tonight…," a hymn our family prayed every evening with our children. A few years after we left seminary, my wife Anne and I lost twin boys at birth. Charlie took the time to write a very loving and caring pastoral note in which he shared thoughts of our common loss.

This was Charlie for me. Truly his name is to be added to the giants in the church he loved and the community in which he lived and served. But, more than that, true giants are real people; and the things I can reflect upon are the human qualities and the affectionate personal touches that he so eloquently added to the theological scholarship that was his life's work.

— Robert D. Schenkel

A Spiritual Mentor
and a True Friend

At a formative time in my life, Charles Price was a spiritual mentor to me and a true friend. His mark on me has been permanent, and I am richer for having known him. I never really thanked Mr. Price for all that he did for me. I regret this now, even as he was not someone who sought or seemed to need the thanks of others. That omission, however, makes me welcome all the more the opportunity to write this reflection.

My first exposure to Charles Price came through listening to his sermons at Memorial Church while I was a Harvard freshman in the fall of 1968. His earnest, direct style of preaching appealed intuitively to me. That period at Harvard was one of intense questioning of the U.S. role in Vietnam and more broadly of all forms of authority, and most undergraduates were on the lookout to ridicule anything hinting of pretentiousness or hypocrisy. Against that backdrop, Mr. Price's sincerity and strength of conviction struck a personal inner chord. His sermons conveyed a sense of struggle to find truth. At a subliminal level, I both identified with that struggle and embraced the expressions of faith it produced, expressions that had undergone trial by fire in Mr. Price's brilliant mind. Each of his sermons rewarded the careful listener. The first part typically laid a foundation for what followed, and a metamorphosis of sorts often occurred at an intermediate point, changing the sermon's trajectory. The sermons were structures of ideas built with powerful intellectual rigor. As I listened, I would often cover my order of service with notes—and I was not the only one.

I began to have direct contact with Mr. Price when I became an usher at Memorial Church. Charles and Betty Price occasionally invited ushers to their home for lunch following the Sunday service, and for dinner at other times. At some point I began to visit Mr. Price in his office as well. Although Harvard in the late 1960s and early 1970s was legendary for offering undergraduates little or no direct contact with professors, Mr. Price was accessible to everyone. While his masterful sermons could be intimidating, he was an easy partner in conversation because he listened intently and was nonjudgmental. To an undergraduate, that counted for a lot. In one conversation about life in the Harvard dorms, I recall him observing with characteristic humor and warmth that he didn't believe people's behavior changed across generations, but rather just the prevailing, socially accepted attitudes toward that behavior. I will never forget complaining to him in another exchange about the custom at Memorial Church of singing "Adeste Fideles" in Latin. He responded that he thought it just sounded better in Latin. At the next Advent service, however, he announced that as a result of a student complaint, the carol would be sung that year in English. I felt empowered and mortified in the same moment. I realized he had been right—in the setting of Memorial Church, "Adeste Fideles" really does sound better in Latin. I subsequently told him so, and the following year it was back to Latin.

Some of my most heartfelt memories of Mr. Price recall the comfort he provided my sister Rebecca and me during the months that preceded her death in the spring of 1972. She had worked as a secretary in Boston, far from our family in West Virginia, and suffered from Hodgkin's Disease. He later conducted her memorial service in the Appleton Chapel, and his homily was unforgettable, helping our mother and the rest of our family deal with our pain and sorrow. In his remarks, Mr. Price made no effort to diminish the tragedy of Rebecca's death or to explain it through references to scripture or "God's will." Rather, he confronted head-on the inexplicable nature of her loss, and asked us to maintain our faith in God to help us endure such a hard time. His points were honest and direct, and he did not attempt to gloss over the stark reality of the moment. By helping us to confront reality, Mr. Price offered the only comfort that was possible, and he helped us to move forward.

Another memory I cherish is a weekend that I spent with Charles and Betty Price at their summer home in the Virginia Tidewater country overlooking Chesapeake Bay. I was working my first job out of college in Washington, D.C., in late 1972 or 1973. In their down-to-earth way, they both made me feel like a member of their family. I still remember the walks together, an afternoon sail in the Bay with Mr. Price, great meals, and embracing hospitality. To a young person at the bottom of the ladder in a large Washington office, this was a special gift.

When I graduated from college, Mr. Price "warned" me not to let the Harvard years be the best of my life. He told me of others he knew who had spent much of their adult years living in the memories of their time as undergraduates at Harvard. I took his admonition seriously, and I'm sure it was one of the factors causing me never really to look back.

The forcefulness of Charles Price's thinking, combined with the strength of his belief in God, set a powerful example in my own life. His exuberant spirit and engaging acceptance of others were hallmarks of his personality. He was remarkably unconcerned with himself, yet he was also someone with a sure sense of his own being and direction. All of these qualities helped to give Mr. Price a quiet charismatic strength.

Mr. Price's uncompromising commitment to service was another striking trait, and it was a major factor, I believe, in his decision to leave Harvard in 1972 so that he could focus his professional efforts on helping to train a new generation of priests at Virginia Seminary. My career has not involved the ministry, but it has taken me in the direction of public service. I head a not-for-profit organization, that helps to build banking systems needed to support market economies in developing and transition countries. While I cannot connect my work directly to Price's influence on me, I believe that his commitment to serving others set a standard that has exerted a subtle pull on me. I am deeply thankful for having known him, and for all that he gave me. His influence has been a guiding force in my life for the last thirty years, and it will continue to be so for as long as I live.

— *J. Andrew Spindler*

They Define for Me
What Resurrection
People Are Like

W<small>HEN</small> I <small>WAS A</small> <small>SEMINARIAN</small>, Charles Price was many things to me. He was the Liturgical Calendar. He was the unlikely pastor. He was common sense in the midst of theological chaos. He was the sacred keeper of ambiguities. He was an entire cheering section of the stadium. His was a face that looked directly into faces. He was an explosion that could wait in silence. His brutal honesty was acceptable because he believed in the best you could give. In those years of seminary, his life was my most important textbook.

In the years of my diaconate, priesthood, and episcopacy, Charles Price has been a standard by which I measured incidents. How would Charlie address this? What if I spelled out all of the issues like Charlie did, could I arrive at a reasonable and faithful conclusion? Would Charlie understand what I am doing? Would he be proud of me? Even now, though he's dead, Charlie tutors me.

Liturgical Calendar—He was the one person at Virginia Seminary who gave us a hint of the wide spectrum of liturgies that we were about to encounter. Being the Bishop of California had forced me to launch far off from Virginia churchmanship.

I learned death and resurrection through the death of Charlie and Betty's daughter and through their passionate suffering as parents. To this day, that funeral pervades my Holy Week wherever I am. They define for me what resurrection people are like.

Unlikely Pastor—I was fortunate enough to have Charlie as my tutor and to spend years with a small group of students in his home knocking about current events from a theological perspective. What we were studying in books has definite application for the real world, and therefore, Charlie kept me grounded. Also, despite his abundant sophistication, students had immediate access to his innocence.

When I was engaged to Mary Willis Taylor of Richmond, Virginia, we clearly needed to have premarital counseling. Obviously we went to Charlie.

Common Sense Amid Theological Chaos—His class outline on the board saved my sanity. So detailed. So approachable. Like a tail that steadies a kite, Charlie's lectures kept the subjects from disappearing into the blowing altitude.

Sacred Keeper of Ambiguities—At lunch or on walks I would be looking for the definitive answer. Charlie was always clear about his personal bias, but he kept the equilibrium by allowing me to see the gravity of both sides. I can see his gestures connoting ambiguity even now.

Cheering Section—Once I wrote a comedy skit and performed it on a community night. Afterwards Charlie ran up to me, grabbed my shoulders, looked widely into my eyes and exclaimed, "I am proud to know you."

An Explosion Waiting in Silence—He would burst into laughter. He played the piano like a volcano ready to erupt. He would berate a latecomer to class in a way that caused everyone to tremble and to respect the theological enterprise. And yet he would sit in wide-eyed silence while your thoughts slowly matured.

Brutally Honest—I remember a paper of mine he graded and on one point remarked, "This isn't right, and even if it were right, it wouldn't make any sense." Once I took a liturgics test, knew it cold, and wrote furiously for the entire three hours. Charlie wrote, "C-, thin."

After seminary I have at least three very vivid memories:

At St. Columba's—I invited Charlie to deliver lectures following our 9:15 a.m. Children and Family Service thirty years ago. We were doing very unorthodox, non-rubrical worship, and I knew it would offend Charlie. After several weeks, Charlie confessed, "I come to St. Columba's each Sunday, and with white knuckles I grip the pew knowing it will drive me crazy. And each Sunday I leave at the end thinking, 'This was terrific.'"

At General Convention—When the new Hymnal 1982 was being decided, Charlie and I were on opposite sides of a debate about "Hark the Herald Angels Sing." Our committee had to come up with final recommendations, and my suggestion prevailed: "…born that we no more may die, born to raise us from the earth, born to give us second birth." Ever since then, when singing Christmas carols, I always think, "Well, Charlie, at least I won one."

United Religions Initiative—When I decided to commit my life to being a catalyst for the creation of a United Religions, there was only one person with whom I wanted to consult: Charlie Price. He assured me that I was on a right track and he gave me his support. That is all I needed.

After forty years of ordained ministry, I am ever so grateful for the quality of Jesus and the Good News that I discerned in Charles Price. There was a groundedness, a freedom, a confidence, an intensity, a gravity, a hilarity, a graciousness that was made transparent in his life. I went to seminary and discovered that it is the Spirit working in our spirits that does the deep teaching. Charlie let the Spirit out!

— *William E. Swing*

Expect the
Reconciliation
of All Things

I ENTERED VTS in the fall of 1958. In those days there were giants at the seminary. I suppose many if not most seminarians feel that way about their teachers, the people who initiated them into the mysteries of the Christian Gospel. For me, Charlie was one of those people.

While I was in junior high school I joined the Episcopal Church and came under the influence of my rector. It was his example that led me to want to become a priest. When people ask me about my career choice I tell them this. I also tell them that initial decision was remade many times and for different reasons.

One of the people responsible for reinforcing that original decision was Charles Price. If my rector taught me what it meant to be a priest, Charlie taught me what it meant to be a Christian. I met Charlie first as a teacher. Later, after ordination, I went to the chaplaincy at Harvard and Radcliff, when he was Preacher to the University at Harvard, and we renewed our acquaintance. During that time Betty, his wife, became godmother to one of my children. Subsequently, I served on the Theological Committee on the Hymnal 1982, which Charlie chaired. By then we had become friends and we remained friends until his death.

Charlie was an example. I believe it was an Old Testament Professor at Virginia Seminary who taught me to see the reading of scripture in particular, and the Christian life in general, in terms of Jacob wrestling with the angel at the brook Jabok. Charlie showed me how it was done. His sermons reflected this struggle, this commitment to be a Christian and to pay the cost, but so did his life. It was Nietzsche who said that if more Christians looked or acted redeemed, he might be persuaded of the truth of the gospel. For me, Charlie showed what it meant to be redeemed in such a way that you wanted to grab hold of his coattails and follow him to find out where he got this extraordinary faithfulness. He was a Christian. You couldn't miss it. He took people seriously. He listened. He engaged people, even people he disagreed with and followed their logic and saw their point and acknowledged their truth as he understood it. He found "sermons in stones and good in everything." He acted as if he was determined to see the world as redeemed the way God saw it; not sinless, redeemed. God, he believed, was committed to the world; therefore, so was he.

Charlie mulled over his sermons all week but he waited until Saturday to set them down in final form. He believed it was important to preach them "hot off the griddle" as he said to me once. That was a habit I admired but could never emulate. (I told him it would be my luck to have the senior warden die that Saturday and to come sermonless to Sunday morning.) Charlie had more faith than I. His sermons conveyed intensity and liveliness. He embraced the anxiety involved in order to better serve.

Yet he was no pollyanna. He was kind enough to come to preach at the 30th anniversary of my ordination and he began his sermon by saying that "Warner Traynham understands sin," a remark that got my congregation's attention. The point was that was where he began his Christian journey, with the human condition squarely-faced. And, he knew that was where I began, too, largely because I had been a student of his. He was anchored in this world but he never lost sight of the fact that his citizenship was in heaven and that he sought a city whose builder and maker was God. Charlie spent himself in the service of the gospel.

He and his wife Betty were for many the pattern of a Christian couple; devoted to one another; aware and appreciative of one another's foibles and loving and accepting still. Their company was always a joy, their faith evident, down-to-earth and sound. They shared a sense of humor that enabled them to see and laugh at the ironies of life and to take life seriously at the same time. Their sorrow was real. Their happiness was real. Their partnership was real. Their faith was real. It all went together.

There was a balance about Charlie, an evenhandedness, a perceptiveness that characterized his being. He inspired trust. He was not first and foremost a partisan. It is a quality rare in the church and rarer still in the world, but Charlie had it. Both the church and the larger society will miss that. I will miss a teacher, a mentor, a friend. But I shall miss him only for a time; for one of the things I learned from him was to expect the reconciliation of all things which, to my mind, includes the restoration of all that here we may have lost.

— *Warner R. Traynham*

Simply a Man Who Has Learned to Live in This World

I‌T WAS ALMOST FORTY YEARS AGO when a Virginia Seminary faculty colleague, Cliff Stanley said at the conclusion of a chapel sermon, "A Christian man is not some strange wonder, fit to set tongues clicking so that perhaps we should charge admission to see him. He is simply a man who has learned to live in this world, not some imaginable one. Quietly he goes about the business, though beset on every side. In the presence of the true 'Thou' he has taken the measure of every memory and afterward says, 'If God be for us, who can be against us?' Because he is a plain man serenely accomplishing the living set before every man to do, his is the best of all ways to be alive; it is the fulfillment of humanity."

Those were the days when for Cliff, as well as for the rest of us, we were almost totally unaware of the exclusivity implied by the word "man." But that didn't lessen the esteem both Cliff and Charlie felt for one another. And what Cliff said in that sermon describes Charlie for me. Charlie was not some strange wonder. He never put on airs. And he never forgot his humanity regardless of his ordination, his graduate degrees, and his positions.

In other words, what I remember most about Charlie was that he never forgot his God-given *humanity*. He didn't let his office or status or role go to his head. I'm not surprised to know he fought *that* demon. After all, being Preacher to the University at Harvard ranks near the top of importance measured by the norms of contemporary culture. I can't imagine that Charlie ever referred to himself or expected others to use the titles, "Father

Price" or "Doctor Price." He believed what Cliff had said in that sermon, "A Christian man is not some strange wonder...."

Of course Charlie was gifted. He was articulate, imaginative, intelligent, and eloquent. But he never forgot his humanity. As far as I am concerned, his faith included his humanity. That embodiment makes Charlie's faith alive and fresh.

As a preacher Charlie was a model for me. I envied him. Not only did he use his gifts as a preacher, what he said was an exposition of a biblical text. What he said in a sermon displayed a familiarity with the ways of the world. Because he lived in the real world and not some imaginary one, he was able to relate the biblical story and his grasp of contemporary society. He understood the Bible in depth and he understood the often opposing currents of national life and thought.

Nowhere is this eclipse more obvious than in a sermon Charlie preached, later printed in the *Seminary Journal* of July 1963. The text was Jeremiah 29:7, "But seek the welfare of the city where I have sent you into exile, and pray to the LORD on its behalf, for in its welfare you will find your welfare."

That sermon is almost contemporary in spite of its years.

In his address delivered in Memorial Church at Harvard on March 3, 2000, The Reverend Peter Gomes noted in the Hymnal 1982 there are as many entries for Charlie Price as there are for Isaac Watts. These are the hymns which Charlie translated "so that the texts in ancient tongues could be sung in a language understood by the people."

Charlie loved hymns. He loved music. And he loved to sing. I can still see Charlie singing in the Seminary Chapel, always with gusto and enthusiasm. And accurately, I'd say. Not only did he bring his own literary gifts into collaboration with other poets, he also composed words *and* music himself: *Landate Pueri* from 1960.

The same Cliff Stanley in May 1963 delivered an appreciation for Charlie when he first left the Seminary to become preacher at Harvard. In that appreciation, Cliff remarked about Charlie's friendliness: "If he had his ups and downs, he managed to deal with them inwardly and to give us only joy."

In many ways Charlie was a private person. Few people know his personal ups and downs. But because he experienced the joy, as well as the pain of life, I believe it made Charlie's faith in the triumph of God's Kingdom stronger, more vigorous, more heroic, and more robust.

Charlie's influence certainly deepened my faith. For that I say simply, "Thank you, Charlie."

— *Perry R. Williams*

Thank God He Has Been Part of Our Lives

Words cannot adequately capture the dynamism that was Charlie Price. I recall arriving at Seminary and seeing a vigorous figure striding across the campus, intently focused on whatever was his next task. I remember thinking that here was someone I wanted to know.

Soon I was seated with the rest of the Junior Class in one of his lectures. I had never known a teacher with such stimulating effect. Charlie was genuinely excited about what he was teaching and the feeling was contagious. I found myself enrolling in whatever electives he was currently teaching, observing to my buddies that if he were teaching basket weaving I would still learn more theology than anywhere else.

In those years there was an institution called "faculty night" when instructors took turns presenting an evening based on something other than their main field. Since Charlie was unbelievably talented in Old and New Testament, as well as music and art, liturgy and preaching, his evenings were always intriguing. I vividly recall one on hymnody, with Charlie illustrating his points by playing piano and singing. It was an invigorating evening. Afterward, Phil Smith was heard to say, "He does everything so darn well. I just wish that once he would fall on his face."

It was in a couples' study group following those presentations that Pat and I first got to know Betty and Charlie on a personal level. There were enjoyable discussions on a variety of topics and Charlie was sincerely interested in our thoughts. It was there I learned that he spent as much time responding to each person's paper or exam as they had spent writing it. That is dedication.

I have never known a teacher who had a more positive effect on me. Yet, it was far more than the content of his lectures. Behind it all was his genuine and transparent faith shining through. This was a faith that was strong enough to be questioned and struggled with and it would still triumph. No silk gloves here, but a strong undergirding foundation.

Since graduating from seminary, I have been fortunate to have had many opportunities to know and appreciate Charlie. He came to Montana to speak at a clergy conference. Since it was being held in an isolated resort, he flew into Billings and then we drove across Montana to the meeting. Never before had he experienced "the wide open spaces." At each turn of the road his interest and enthusiasm showed. "But where," he asked, "are all of the people?" I doubt there was ever a time when he wasn't observing and learning.

Years later when I attended the continuing education program at Virginia Seminary, Charlie was one of the presenters. I was gratified to see how excited fellow students were with his innovative and stimulating thoughts. As always, he was dynamic and powerful—like a breath of fresh air.

Yet it was at General Convention that he had his greatest effect on the broader Church. His contributions to the development of both the Prayer Book and Hymnal were vital. Not only was his scholarship important, his ability to get along with others and to help them work together was critical. At one time or another he served as Chaplain to both Houses of General Convention. Add this to his many publications, and one can see that his influence on the Church has been significant.

Yet, for me personally, Charlie was most important as a sensitive, caring friend. When I was ordained bishop, Charlie traveled west again, to a very wintry Spokane, to preach an exciting sermon—helping the diocese and me to move into a new chapter. When Charlie was with you he was totally with you—never looking over your shoulder at something else.

We all miss him and his unselfish contributions. But thank God he has been part of our lives.

— *Leigh Wallace*

Each of Us Will
Never Be the Same

THERE IS ONLY ONE THING unusual about the invitation to write about Charles Price: since I have Charlie in mind so many times in so many ways, sitting down to write about him seemed a different discipline to follow. As one of his legion of students (and admirers), I have written *for* him on many occasions, but this is different. It is daunting, for one struggles to find the right words to convey that vitality of heart, spirit, and mind that was truly remarkable.

While it may seem a superficial thing to note when thinking of such a keen intellect, I cannot escape the first thought to come to my mind: Has anyone ever laughed with such great gusto? In fact, has anyone ever sung hymns with such true enthusiasm? Has anyone ever conveyed a deeper sense of mystery in telling the Good News? Charlie would not countenance all these high-blown praises, but his friends all know the truth of these memories.

In my last semester at Virginia Seminary, Charlie agreed to do an independent study course with me. We set out to familiarize ourselves with the writings of the great William Porcher DuBose. For me this was in part a patriotic duty, for DuBose and I are both South Carolinians by birth. In fact, my great-great-grandfather baptized DuBose. For Charlie this was an overdue study, as he put it, for in all his long career he had not addressed himself to the considerable body of DuBoses's work. So we set a course which was demanding in every sense of the word. There was much to read in a limited time, and even more to ponder. Charlie approached this with more enthusiasm than I could have imagined (or demonstrated). Aside from whatever content we gleaned from those studies, I saw in Charlie's example the true scholar, the scholar who maintains a deep enthusiasm for the academic discipline being pursued, one to whom learning "afresh"—one of Charlie's favorite words—was a joy to be cherished.

There was a certain Wednesday in Holy Week, when the seminary was gathered for Holy Eucharist in the Chapel. Charlie was the preacher, and he addressed the topic of evil. Judas was the central figure in his sermon, and when he came to the line from St. John, "And it was night" (John 13:30), Charlie's delivery made it clear to one and all that something dreadful had just happened. His hearers had to know that he had captured the absolute essence of what the Evangelist meant to say. We could feel it in a palpable way. The power of the preacher was never greater.

I have a letter from Charlie, written in 1988 when he and Betty were on sabbatical in England. In it he recounts an Easter Day sermon he heard, one in which he spent a good deal of time in confusion because he had not properly understood the preacher's words. [Charlie had mistaken "badger" for

"Thatcher." You can imagine the confused context from that point on.] The reason I love the letter, aside from the comic account of an Easter Day, was Charlie's absolute delight in humor at his own expense, his willingness to share it and the way he eventually tied it all together with a suitable theological analysis. In one personal letter were so many of those sterling attributes we loved: Clear insight, clear faith in the Resurrection and just the right touch of humor to provide the graceful leaven of the moment.

A cherished and deeply personal memory: I happened to be at the hospital the night Charlie died. Betty had told me earlier that day that I should come by. When I came near to his room, it was clearly evident he was dying. Betty, their grandson Philip, and Phil and Barbara Smith, dear friends, were at his bedside. I felt like an interloper, and, catching Betty's eye, I just waved and turned to leave. Betty told the nurse to ask me to stay, but I stood outside Charlie's room. In a few minutes, he died.

Not long after, we were all taken back into his room where Phil asked me to lead prayers. I was overwhelmed, to think of leading prayers for Charlie, from whom I had learned so much about Anglican worship. Then I remembered something he once said about the rubrics, namely that it was okay to break one on two conditions. First, it was necessary to know what the rubric intended in the first place, and, second, there had to be very good reason. With that I was able to know the grace all worship leaders must have in any circumstance, and I thus received one of the rarest privileges and gifts I could ever hope to know.

There is a common theme in these pieces. It is how each of us will never be the same after knowing Charlie. Simply put, to be introduced to so much that really matters, to be challenged in ways of thinking and trying to preach the Gospel, and to be in the company of such a friend—all that and more came from knowing him. Those changes live on in everyone who came into his company, and who shares the life of the One whom Charlie served so well.

— *William M. Shand*

Non Nobis Domine

An address delivered in
The Memorial Church, Harvard
University on March 3, 2000
in thanksgiving for the life and work
of Charles P. Price

Nοτ LONG AFTER HIS FAREWELL SERMON as
Preacher to the University, an article about
Charles Price was published in the *Boston
Globe*. The title was: "Harvard's Quiet Voice
in a Troubled Time." That was 1972, and it
had been a very troubled time. Much of the

trouble I have forgotten. But the quiet voice in the midst of it I remember, and always will.

That was his way, that troubled Sunday and always: To begin, not with what he personally might have been feeling, not with thoughts that had happened to occur to him, but to begin with the Word, to rely on something beyond himself, to take his stand on wisdom and authority greater than his own. He couldn't avoid being in the public eye. That went with the job. He could, and did, direct the attention away from himself. That was his way: a kind of humbleness that had in it nothing at all of pretense.

That was his way, and it explains why so much of the good he did, here and elsewhere, was done as if it were by stealth. He was adept at letting not the left hand know what the right hand doeth. He was closely involved, for example, in the making of both the books by which his own Church now conducts its worship: the Hymnal 1982 and The Book of Common Prayer. In the Hymnal, there are as many entries for Charles Price as there are for Isaac Watts himself. But you have to look for them, because not one of those entries is a hymn entirely his own. There are hymns he translated, so that texts in ancient tongues could be sung in a language "understanded of the people." There are hymns he added stanzas to, which enlarge their meaning and bring sentiments of the past into the present. In short, he brought his own literary gifts into collaboration with other poets, so that the church (like the scribe in the Gospel) might bring out of its treasure things old and new at once.

Not that he would have put it so. *His* way of saying what I have just said was: "I have taken a new job. I'm employed as a hymn-adjuster."

He used to joke in the same self-effacing way about his contribution to The Book of Common Prayer. "The thing in the Prayer Book," he said, "the one thing in the Prayer Book that I should be remembered for is the Price Comma."

What he called the Price Comma is in the Nicene Creed—the greatest Christian hymn of all, you might say. The Prayer Book was to have a new wording of the Creed, and Charles insisted (quietly, I'm sure) that there is one place where the meaning of this new translation depends on how it is punctuated. So a comma was added, the Price Comma; and there it is, in the clause about God the Maker of heaven and earth. It is a very small thing, but very typical; because what that comma does, unmistakably, is shift the emphasis of the clause, so that instead of falling on us, on those who may or may not see what has been created, the emphasis falls on God who creates.

There you have Charles Price. The theme of his whole ministry was the Psalm that begins, "Not unto us, O Lord, not unto us, but unto thy Name give the praise" (Ps. 115, *Non Nobis Domine*).

And to be sure he did contribute more, much more than punctuation to The Book of Common Prayer. He helped to give it the *thankfulness* that is its keynote. Running all through its pages is an invitation to perceive "all that is, seen and unseen," the world of nature, and especially the world of human living, joys and disappointments alike—to perceive it all as it most truly is: a gift, as the outward and visible sign of a generosity for which "it is right, and a good and joyful thing, always and everywhere to give thanks." That was Charles's theology. It was the theology he aspired to live. It was the theology of his preaching.

And, it was the theology he taught. He was my teacher, the first teacher of theology I had, and the best. When as an undergraduate I had taken all the formal lecture courses he offered, Charles directed an independent study project, and once a week or so I would have an hour with him to discuss what I was reading. I kept a journal then, and there is an entry about those meetings.

Usually they were in the late afternoon. Mr. Price (I wrote) would be tired, after a day full of responsibilities, and he would *look* tired when I arrived. And that lasted about ten minutes. Once he started talking about theology—about eucharistic presence, or the coinherence of the Trinity, or Hooker's idea of the church, or any of those specialist topics that theologians delight in—then his whole demeanor changed, and his eyes lit up, and he would bounce in his chair—you might not picture the Preacher to the University bouncing in his chair but he did—because he loved what he was doing. He loved the subject matter, and he loved teaching it.

And, as always, he declined to cast himself in the starring role. He would finish explaining some deep and difficult point, and make everything admirably clear, and I would think, "Good. Now I really understand that." And Mr. Price would say: "Now. That's what *I* think. But I've not done justice to the such-and-such point of view." So we would start the same topic all over from a different angle.

If you wanted sharp-edged, black-and-white, yes-or-no answers, Charles was not the man to go to. He was too fair-minded. Truth is one, but it has more than one side, and he was too honest—and too Anglican—to smooth out the complexities.

If I were asked to say what was most important in all that I learned from him, I would not point to any of those careful answers. They were full of insights that were well worth learning. But Charles's answers were all of them answers to one question. This was the question that made him a theologian, and a question worth making one's own. He put it this way: "I've devoted a big part of my life," he said, "to finding out how one might go about being, at one and the same time, an intelligent human being, and a Christian."

One way or another, it was that question he faced so fairly, and struggled with so honestly, and answered in that quiet voice, over and over, time after time, as a professor of theology, as a preacher of the Word, as a person—a very intelligent human being, and a faithful, humble Christian.

The article I mentioned at the outset closes in good journalistic fashion with a pithy quotation. I can't better it, so I borrow it. The dean of one of the graduate schools told the reporter: "Charles Price was a powerful person. Not in the sense that he was a charismatic man...but in the sense that he consistently touched one or two dozen people in ways that they will never be the same."

So he did. Thanks be to God.

— *Charles C. Hefling, Jr.*

Don Clark, "Rev. Charles Price: Harvard's Quiet Voice in a Troubled Time," *The Boston Globe*, 8 July 1972. The quotation above is attributed to Lawrence E. Fouraker, then dean of the Business School.